Me, Myself & Intuition
Managing Your Psychic Gift

Books by Miss Dee

Me, Myself & Intuition

The Best of Miss Dee

From Fire to Flight

Health, Astrology & Spirituality

The Yod, Your Special Life Purpose

Me, Myself & Intuition
Managing Your Psychic Gift

Miss Dee

Me, Myself & Intuition
Managing Your Psychic Gift

© Copyright 2017 by Miss Dee

Cover Art and Illustrations:
Robert & Margaret Carspecken www.ozfoxes.com and Miss Dee

Cover Design, Copy Editor, Interior Layout: Jennifer Sweete

Content Editor: Hal

Paperback
13 ISBN: 978-0-9992196-0-7
10 ISBN: 0-9992196-0-X

1st Edition, 2017

Printed in the United States of America

Dedication

Dedicated to you, my psychic companions, to help you know the truth about you, which is that you are psychic/sensitive/intuitive persons blessed with a gift, not a curse . . . that you are special, and if the truth be known—revered; and most importantly, that you can manage or control your psychic gift.

With my sincerest thanks to

Mike, my husband, whose belief in and encouragement of me never ceased.

Hal, my content editor, whose eagle eyes and sharp and inquiring mind suggested alternative phrases and words, but most of all, for his "bottom of my heart" support.

Robert and Margaret, my illustrators, whose amazing talents with pen and ink brought to paper the images I saw in my head, and for "being here for you."

Jennifer Sweete, my go-to gal, whose help I could not have done without.

Table of Contents

Introduction for All Ages

Once upon a time, when I was six or seven years old, I was a lot like you. I saw people like you see people—glowing, radiant with many colors. I also saw those "other" people who looked either soft and feathery or dark and mysterious.

Sometimes, when I let them talk to me, their lips did not move but I could hear them talking. At other times, some of those "other" people were scary or frightening because they were very large and very dark. I did not know what they wanted or why they were there because I was too frightened to ask. Instead, I would cover my head with my blanket or run out of the room!

Like you, I knew about events that were going to happen, and I even knew how they were going to turn out. And sometimes, I knew someone's secret even though no one had told me the secret. But I did not know how I knew these things.

Like you, sometimes when I was with someone, I was suddenly afraid or angry or confused, and I was sure that I was not in that type of mood before I spent some time with this person! Feeling other people's different emotions would sometimes happen when I was alone.

I was shy. I did not like being around people and wished I could just be like everyone else. I knew I was different, but I did not know what to do to be like other people, or who to talk to, or even what questions to ask.

For what seemed to be a long time, I did not know I was psychic. I just knew I was different, and that made me very unhappy.

Many, many years later, I met a very nice woman. Her name was Jacqueline and she was psychic. She could see, sense, and feel that I was unhappy, painfully shy, and fearful because of the visions or mental pictures and the "other" people I was seeing, the voices of who-knows-whom I was hearing, and the bombardment of emotions constantly assaulting my senses.

Jacqueline explained to me that I was psychic. I knew the word and what it meant because I had been told before that I was psychic. The previous times I received this same message I felt peaceful. This time, along with the peacefulness I felt, in my head I heard beautiful bells ringing and then my tummy finally relaxed so I could take in a really deep breath of air!

After I exhaled my deep breath of air, Jacqueline explained to me that it was because I was psychic that I felt different or alone, that I picked up or felt other people's emotions, and that my "third eye" (All Seeing Eye) was open, which is why I knew things without being told.

Well, you can imagine! I finally had some clarity about having the psychic gift. Being sensitive to other people's emotions and knowing things beforehand was the psychic gift in action. While I was in a state of awe with my new understanding and wondering what, if anything, I was suppose to do with knowing things ahead of time, Jacqueline must have read my mind. She interrupted my thoughts with an offer to help me understand, and then, if I chose to, use my gift. Well naturally, I gratefully accepted!

Even if you are over the age of seven or eight, I hope you will accept my invitation to read the chapters: "The Magical Self," "The Psychic Self," and "A Note from the Author" in Part 1.

"The Magical Self," will introduce you to auras, the colored light that sometimes appears around people. Knowing you are seeing orange, lavender, or some other color around a person may be a confusing or frightening experience for you, but need not be scary anymore.

"The Psychic Self," a touch-on-lightly piece, was written to help psychic children empower themselves, and it can get the ball of empowerment rolling for you, too.

Lastly, you may find "A Note from the Author"—a note written to the parents/guardians of a psychic child—a heartwarming and eye-opening piece. It may send you back into your childhood for a short time. If it does, give yourself a big hug and then wrap a pink blanket of compassion around you, because once upon a time, you were that child.

In my heart of hearts, I would like you to know the truth about you, so you understand why you feel you are different and know the things you know without anyone telling you.

I would like you to be unafraid of the soft and feathery people and the dark and mysterious people who talk to you.

Most of all, I would like you to learn how to take charge of your psychic gift instead of letting it control you.

I wrote this book to help you to know the truth about you: that you are psychic and that your gift is manageable.

With love, *Miss Dee*

Part 1

The Psychic Child

For ages up to about seven years old

A Note from the Author

To the Parents/Guardians of a Psychic Child,

I understand that you may feel as fearful and as frustrated with the strange things that happen to your child as he/she does. I wrote this book to help clear up the terror, confusion, and helplessness you may feel and watch your child go through.

You may not see the dark and mysterious figure or large person or people that your child sees—and those are frightening sights for a child.

You may not see the quick movement of something out of the corner of your eye, or see in your mind a wispy-figured person in the doorway or at a window.

You may not know about a coming event—someone becoming gravely ill, for example—but your child does. Not only does your psychic child know about the person's illness, but also whether that person will live or die.

Your child knows about your deceased great aunt and her well-guarded indiscretions, and this is certainly something you would not have told your child.

You may not hear in your mind someone saying something to you, something you do not understand, or see someone showing you a picture of something you cannot make out clearly.

You may not, suddenly and for no reason at all, get nervous, anxious, angry, frustrated, or fearful. Or suffer headaches from the barometric pressure falling, or from an earthquake occurring halfway across the world. Or tuck a second hankie into your pocket "because you need it," and hours later, you have a bloody nose and do need it!

And you may not feel different from your peers, painfully different or alone, even in a roomful of people.

These are many of the experiences of a psychic child. I know because at the very tender age of six or seven I was doing or experiencing some of these very same unearthly things. But my first and most vivid recollection of my gift, although I did not know that it was a gift, was the knowing that someone very dear to me was terribly ill and no one would believe me!

To make a long story short, this wonderful woman was ill and getting worse. This woman and her spouse tried very hard to keep it a secret from me and other people close to her. As a result, I was being nurtured in an atmosphere charged with secrecy and that left me feeling confused about what I saw, which was entirely different from what I felt and knew in my heart to be true. To say the least, I had a difficult psychic childhood!

To add to the difficulty, no one in my family, on either side, showed the signs of having the gift, so there was no one who could help me. Thankfully, when I was around the age of twenty-eight, I was blessed with Jacqueline, a psychic who became my mentor. She knew the agony, confusion, and fear I was experiencing. She knew I thought I was different—not special, just different— maybe even heading into the realm of being crazy.

It was Jacqueline and a few other wonderful psychics who taught me that I could turn off the visitations from those dark and mysterious or soft and wispy figures, and turn away from the pictures they tried to show me, at least for a period of time. They taught me that I could block unwanted energies or un-become the very uncomfortable emotional sponge that psychics or sensitive/intuitive children and grown-ups experience being.

With practice, a lot of practice on my part actually, and staying centered in my heart, I learned that being psychic was and is truly a gift, that I am as normal as you are except that I know things you may not know and see things you may not see, and that this very special gift is manageable.

"The Magical Self" (Chapter 1) is a fun story about how a red planet explodes. In the process, it deposits its beautiful golden light into everyone and, as each person scatters into space, he/she chooses a color to wear like a coat. This story gives emphasis to your child's uniqueness and beauty within (the shimmering golden inner light), and it teaches your child about auras, the colored light around people. Knowing you are different from your peers and seeing red, green, or some other color around a person can be frightening or confusing experiences for a child.

"The Psychic Self" (Chapter 2), a touch-on-lightly piece, is written to help psychic children understand and use their gift, to teach them how to protect themselves from the emotions and the visions or pictures that can bombard them, and to teach them how to manage their gift, which is empowering.

"The Gift of Being Psychic" (Chapter 3) and "Some of My Experiences" (Chapter 4) will help you understand what your child is experiencing. I hope these chapters will encourage you to support your child as he/she practices shielding and centering and becoming efficient at both, and help you to be patient with your child as his/her learning continues by the use of the techniques of shutting down—or "pausing"—the psychic gift and, if your child chooses, opening it up again.

With the warmest wishes, *Miss Dee*

Chapter 1
The Magical Self

O nce, but only once, upon a time, a very, very, *very* long time ago, there was a gigantic red planet.

Not only was this planet gigantic, it was huge. It was enormous! It was humongous because it was full of wonderfully marvelous things.

These wonderfully marvelous things bounced around in a mysterious golden liquid that twinkled as if it were full of stars. This mysterious golden liquid lived in the very center of the humongous red planet.

The wonderfully marvelous things, which bounced around in the mysterious golden liquid, were love, kindness, and sympathy, happiness, creativity, and courage.

Also bouncing around in the mysterious golden liquid were laughter, helpfulness, and lots of other good things.

Well, as all of these wonderfully marvelous things bounced around inside the humongous red planet, they duplicated themselves with each bounce.

They kept duplicating themselves; and before too long, some rips and tears began to occur in the skin of the humongous red planet. After a very long time, the humongous red planet simply could not hold any more.

Well, do you know what happened?

KAA-BOOOM!

It exploded!

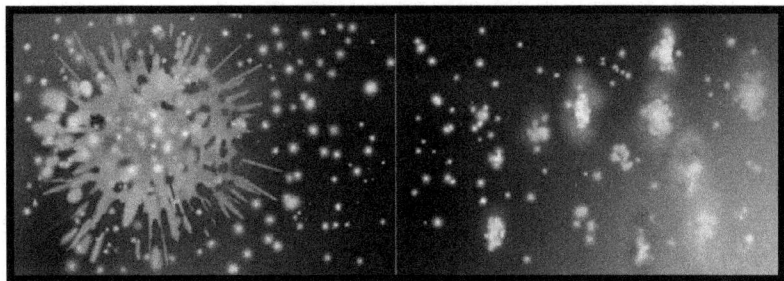

In a split second, all of the many wonderfully marvelous things that had been bouncing around inside the humongous red planet were suddenly hurled far out into space.

Well, you can just imagine how surprised all of those many wonderfully marvelous things must have been!

As soon as they got their wits about them, they grabbed each other's hands and began to form the most beautiful, colorful spheres like bubbles around the splashes and splotches of that mysterious golden liquid.

Each wonderfully marvelous thing chose a color to wrap the bubble or itself in. Love chose what she thought was the most beautiful color, which was green. Kindness chose to be white. Sympathy chose to be a golden color similar to the mysterious golden liquid, just a lighter shade. Happiness chose blue. Creativity chose orange. Courage chose to be red, laughter chose yellow, and helpfulness chose violet. And the wonderfully marvelous thing called *Intuition* chose to be the color purple.

Well, some of the color spheres joined hands with other color spheres and became different shades of white, blue, yellow, orange, gold, red, violet, green, and purple. Next, even more of the color spheres joined hands with other color spheres to become other different and beautiful shades of color, which were still the wonderfully marvelous things, like love and laughter, though now they wore a coat or a wrap of one, two, or many colors. Do you know why?

Because a long time from that "Once upon a time," some people would wrap themselves in a coat, or dress, or blanket of the colors they like. Now when people put on that coat or wrap, they will feel the wonderfully marvelous things that the color or colors are vibrating! They will feel happy, courageous, loving, creative, kind, sympathetic, and psychic/sensitive/intuitive. Remember, the colors are the wonderfully marvelous things, like love and happiness wrapped around the splashes and splotches of that mysterious golden liquid!

People who put on a coat or a wrap of blue, for example, will be happy or use their happiness to help other people be happy. Or, if a person chooses to wear a coat or a wrap of yellow and green, that person will be happy and loving. And if a person puts on a coat or a wrap of purple, that person will be intuitive or use their intuition to help them throughout their entire life, and may also help other people by the use of intuition.

"Once upon a time" it was exciting, very exciting to watch each colorful wonderfully marvelous thing sparkle and shimmer as they all encircled that mysterious golden liquid that twinkled as if it were full of stars.

But wait! I haven't told you what that mysterious golden liquid is, have I?

It is the Magical Self! And it lives inside the center of your heart!

And do you know what lives *inside* the Magical Self, which lives inside the center of your heart?

Four things . . .

THE FIRST thing is all of the power you will ever need to help you make your dreams come true.

THE SECOND thing is a huge library full of all of the knowledge and wisdom you will ever need to help you make your dreams come true.

THE THIRD thing is intuition. Intuition is something like a telephone that you can use to talk to your power or ask your power to help you. Intuition is also something like a television screen where anything you want to understand, or see, or learn from the huge library will appear on the screen whenever you ask it to show you.

THE FOURTH thing that lives inside the Magical Self is the combination of three Goodnesses: bravery, honesty, and thoughtfulness.

All four of these things live inside the Magical Self, which lives inside the center of your heart, making the beautiful golden liquid twinkle as if it were full of stars.

Remember when the humongous red planet exploded because it could not hold any more of the wonderfully marvelous things and all the golden liquid?

Well, it seemed that the only way to set the beautiful golden liquid free in order for it to get into and then live inside a person's heart, was for the humongous red planet to explode. So it did!

Now some of that beautiful golden liquid lives inside *your* Magical Self, which lives inside the center of *your* heart!

It is both—the beautiful golden liquid that lives inside your Magical Self, which lives inside the center of your heart, and the purple coat or wrap of intuition— that makes you so very special.

You, unlike most people, know about coming events or things that are going to happen that no one has told you about. You see things and/or people-shapes that many other people do not see. And you feel different emotions or energies that some other people do not feel! All of these things, which come to you through your intuition, are called the psychic gift and you have it, and that is really special!

You are what some people call "sensitive" or "intuitive," or a person who listens to and uses their intuition. You are what some people call psychic. And being psychic is very special!

Chapter 2
The Psychic Self

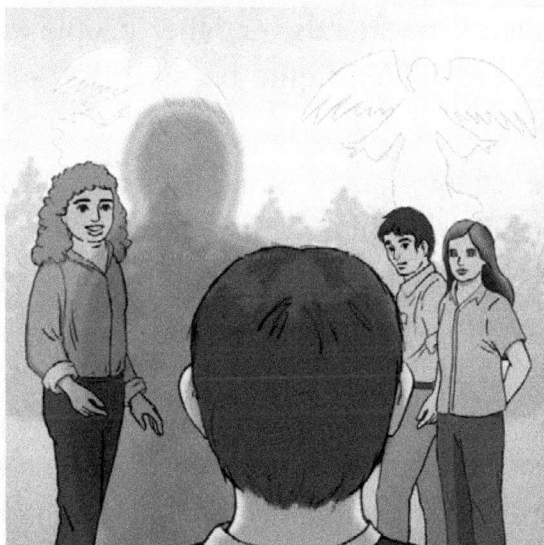

Inside your Magical Self, which lives inside the center of your heart, is a very, very special gift. It is the gift of being psychic—intuitive or sensitive. This gift is precious, as are you, my luv.

Did you know that when some people look at you, they see that beautiful golden liquid twinkling and spinning around you? Yes, they know that there is something special about you, something wonderfully different! That is why some people smile at you, just like the three people in the picture at the beginning of this chapter are smiling at the little boy because they see that beautiful golden liquid twinkling and spinning around him.

Not all people who look at you will see that beautiful golden liquid twinkling and spinning around you, and that's OK. These people, perhaps some of your classmates, or friends, or other people you know may not see the golden liquid because they *choose* not to see it. Why?

Because they have already shut down their psychic/sensitive/intuitive gift since they do not understand it or are frightened by it. Something important to remember is this: everyone is born with the psychic gift, but not everyone chooses to use it. That is why when some people look at you, they do not see that beautiful golden liquid twinkling and spinning around you. Other people, who *do* see that beautiful golden liquid, know that there is something special about you, something wonderfully different.

You are intuitive, sensitive, or psychic; and being intuitive, sensitive, or psychic means that you are special!

You are so special because you can see Angels and Protectors. The Protectors are usually very large people-like figures, and sometimes look like very dark shadows, and seem to be almost invisible but are not. They are bigger than an adult, and can look scary or be very frightening.

But their name, "Protectors," explains what they do: they protect you and me and other people. They keep a watchful eye on us and help keep us safe. The picture in this chapter, which is the same drawing as is on the cover of this book, is a picture of a Protector. He is on the right side of the little boy. The little boy is looking at the Protector who is very large and looks like a dark shadow, and seems to be almost invisible but is not.

Now that you know that these "other" people who are almost invisible or perhaps look like very dark shadows, are your Protectors, you no longer need to be afraid of them. But if you still are, you can tell them in a very firm voice to leave you alone and they will.

Being intuitive, sensitive, or psychic means that you are special—*so* special that you can see colors around people. These colors are called auras. Remember when each of the wonderfully marvelous things—like love and helpfulness—chose a color? Love chose green and helpfulness chose violet. Well, each person has also chosen a color to wear like a coat or a wrap. Those colors around people are called auras, but not everyone will see auras. You probably do, and that is special.

You are special because you can talk to animals or talk to plants, and they will talk back to you. And that is really special.

And you are special because you can feel the barometric pressure falling, which tells you a rain or snowstorm is coming into the area where you live. Lots of people don't feel that, but you do!

When the barometric pressure is falling, you may start feeling different. You might feel anxious, nervous, or jittery, and you may feel as if a heavy book is sitting on your head. These energies probably make you uncomfortable, but now that you know this is a feeling message from your intuition, you can thank your intuition for the feeling message and then ask it to stop the uncomfortable feelings. And it will, but it will not stop the rain or snowstorm! Remember, asking your intuition to stop or turn off the uncomfortable feelings is OK.

Being intuitive, sensitive, or psychic, means you are so special that you can see pictures in your head—pictures of something that is going to happen, like a big snowstorm, for example. In your picture, the snow covers everything, and there is so much of it that an adult cannot walk through it. That is a picture of a blizzard.

What is so special about you seeing this picture is that you can tell your Mom, Dad, Guardian, or someone else you trust about the picture you saw and they may decide to heed your psychic forewarning and prepare for bad weather by going to the store to get a few groceries.

Being intuitive, sensitive, or psychic, means you are so special that you often hear a voice in your head, a soft voice some people call a "wee small voice." It gives you guidance or instruction like "call your friend" or "don't go" somewhere after school with your friends.

This voice is your intuition, and listening to it and following its instructions is a special and a good habit to develop. A lot of people hear their soft voice or "wee small voice," but they ignore it and later wish they had done what their "wee small voice" had advised them to do.

Your intuition loves you, protects you, and will help you throughout your entire life . . . as long as you listen to it and follow its instructions.

Did you know that your intuition will tell you that someone else is sad or angry so you do not have to be sad or angry when you really are not? All you have to do is ask "who is sad?" or "who is angry?" Your intuition will answer you by whispering the person's name to you, or showing you in your mind a picture of the person who is sad or angry. Asking your intuition for an answer is OK because that helps you manage your gift of being intuitive, sensitive, or psychic.

Sometimes when other people talk to each other and you are close by, you may see different shades of the color red around them. Their voices become louder and louder and then you may start to become angry and then confused. Do you know why? Because they are telling you that they are only talking peacefully when you can clearly see that they are really arguing or disagreeing about something.

Do you know what to do? Yes, ask your intuition if one or both of these people are angry, and it will give you the answer. Then ask your Angels to stand beside you or in front of you and cover you with their wings and they will! And when they do, you will not have to be angry when you really are not, or confused because you see one thing but are being told something different.

Do you know what to do if someone tells you he/she has and uses the psychic gift? Ask your intuition and it will give you the answer. Your intuition may show you this person's beautiful golden liquid twinkling and spinning around him/her. Your intuition may speak to you in its "wee small voice" and whisper something like, "Yes, that is true."

But if this person is not using his/her psychic gift, your intuition will tell you that, too. Your intuition may make your tummy feel tight, or make you feel as if you want to run away. If either of these things happens, or if you feel uncomfortable, tell the person you have to leave; then walk away and ask your Angels to walk behind you and cover you with their wings. They will.

Did you know that your intuition will tell you anything you want to know, because it is connected to that huge library full of all of the knowledge and wisdom you will ever need? And remember, that library lives inside the Magical Self, which lives inside the center of your heart.

Knowledge and wisdom will help you understand why you might be frightened or confused; why you might feel angry or sad when there is no reason to feel angry or sad; and their instruction will help you make your dream come true, whatever your dream is.

Do you remember that you already have all of the power you will ever need to help you? That power also lives inside the Magical Self, which lives inside the center of your heart. If a slimy, yucky, bad, or negative-feeling, almost invisible person is talking to you or standing next to you, your power is so strong and brave that you can firmly tell that person to leave you alone or go away, or that you are busy right now and don't have time to talk.

Being intuitive, sensitive, or psychic, means you are special and precious, my luv—*so* wonderfully special that you understand a picture given to you by your Protector or an Angel or your intuition. And you tell your Mom, Dad, Guardian, or someone else you trust about the picture. You can turn off the switch and not be angry or sad when you really are not; and you can succeed at anything to which you set your heart and mind.

You are wonderfully different because you are intuitive, sensitive, or psychic. Remember, some of that beautiful golden liquid lives inside your Magical Self, which lives inside the center of your heart. And in the very center of your Magical Self is a very, very special gift—the gift of being intuitive, sensitive, or psychic. That gift is very, very special as are you, my luv. And I urge you to let your golden liquid light of specialty shine!

Every morning when you wake up, ask that Angels surround you, protect you, and keep you safe this day; then feel the flutter of their beautiful wings hugging you.

Part 2

The Gift

Chapter 3
The Gift of Being Psychic

For me, being psychic is truly a gift, an amazing, valuable, wonderful gift, a gift I am grateful I learned how to manage. I did not always think this way. I used to think as some people do, that I was losing my marbles!

But, as I learned about my gift and later counseled and taught astrology, metaphysics, and how to manage the psychic gift, people would confide in me that they had the same concerns I had years and years ago.

Those concerns are similar to, "I think I'm losing my mind—what with seeing dark and mysterious figures lurking in the corner and sometimes seeing soft and wispy figures out of the corner of my eye!" Or, "I think I need to get my vision tested because of the shadows and movement of things I see." Or, "Maybe I need to get my hearing tested. I keep hearing noises, like the saltshaker being moved, and voices (though I don't always understand what is being said)."

But, after talking more with each person, it would become apparent that he/she had the psychic gift. After passing on this exciting news to him/her (which more often than not is already known by this person), I hear this:

"A gift? It feels more like a curse!"

Yes, it does feel like a curse until you understand what being psychic/sensitive/intuitive is, and learn to manage it. When you learn to manage it, it does become a gift!

I, too, thought I was losing my marbles, felt I had been cursed and made into an emotional sponge, soaking up other people's anxieties or nervousness. I wondered if my emotions had gone wacky; that I just did not belong in the junior high school I was in, and would never fit in at any school or with any group of kids. I was picked on and bullied because I was different. I knew I was different, and I was withdrawn and lacked confidence because of being different.

I asked myself the same questions you probably ask yourself: *Why do I see shadows of people out of the corner of my eye? Why do I see someone standing three feet above the ground, but no one else does? Why do I see that very large, dark yet transparent person in the corner, but no one else does?*

Why do I see the word "March" in the color of blazing orange, sitting on a fluffy, white cloud? Why do I see dozens of small, perfectly shaped hearts when a particular couple, deeply in love, look at each other, but no one else sees the hearts?

Even worse, *Why do I feel another person's nervousness, anxiety, or sorrow when I am standing near him/her?* Or, *Why do I feel like I was just told a lie?*

Why do I hear a soft, kind voice or a firm, male-type voice telling me to leave five minutes early, take a different route, look left, or buy this and not that?

I know all of these questions and many, many more because I have asked them and have been asked these same and other questions. My answer to you is that you have the gift! You are psychic/sensitive/intuitive!

When I realized this truth about myself, around the age of six or seven, there was a long moment of silence followed by the greatest feeling of peace. I believe the peace came from knowing that I was not crazy. I did not understand what being psychic was; I just knew I was not crazy. And, when my friends and clients heard that they had the gift, there was, once again, that beautiful moment of peace. Perhaps you, too, are experiencing it now.

So, what is psychic or being psychic, and how do you handle it so it does not control you? First, the word "psychic" means to discern, or having the ability to tell the difference between souls or spirits and living people; between a future happening and a past event; between another person's wishful thinking and what will actually transpire; and between your emotions and someone else's emotions.

Being psychic is a wondrous gift, so calling it a curse dishonors the gift and the gift-giver or God, the Universe, or whom or whatever you believe your source to be.

Think about it . . . God is love and His gifts are created from love.

Like it or not, experience teaches us that we have chosen to have and use this gift. Before incarnating into this life or becoming flesh, you chose to have, understand, and manage this wondrous gift. Why would you give yourself a gift you could not use?

Just to clarify who did the choosing of this wonderful and special gift, remember this—the gift of being psychic/sensitive/intuitive is an honor. Yes, it is. Before you incarnated into this life, you and God talked. And the two of you had so much confidence in your talents and abilities, your aptitude and willingness to draw on your vast spiritual wisdom, your integrity of heart, and the life path you two had chosen for you, that God blessed you with the psychic gift—the ability to discern. What you do with it now is up to you.

God also gave you a tool to use—a "hotline" or a telephone line, so to speak, that allows direct communication between the two of you. This "hotline" is the tube, for lack of a better word, that your intuition, guidance, inspiration, and wisdom come through into your consciousness. Looking at your Spiritual body, it is the sixth chakra—Brow or "third eye" chakra—or energy center, which is associated with seeing visions or pictures and hearing the higher voice of intuition. Chapter 6, "The Chakras," explains the chakras or spiritual energy centers, in depth.

How do you know if it is your intuition, wisdom, or guidance coming through your "hotline" tube? Easy. It is unmistakable! It is soft and gentle. It does not shout, condemn, threaten, or frighten. It uses only a few words, but words that are very precise—such as, "blizzard," "three o'clock," or "don't." It is often referred to as the "wee small voice."

You may receive pictures of inspiration or guidance through your "hotline." These pictures will be crystal-clear and momentary.

Accompanying the pictured or heard message, instruction, guidance, or wisdom that comes through your "hotline" is a feeling that relaxes you or some part of your body, gives you a sense of relief, or brings you peace.

If someone tells you that he/she is psychic, or "God told me to tell you," trust the feeling you are experiencing in your stomach or gut area. This area is the third chakra—or Solar Plexus chakra—located around the navel. It is referred to as the seat of knowingness or "feeling the truth." This is where many people, including a psychic/sensitive/intuitive person such as you, will feel, or sense, or have a "gut instinct" feeling that this person either is trying to deceive you or is giving you a sincere message, or that he/she is either a genuine psychic or a charlatan.

Before you go any further, it's a good idea to think about these things . . .

Of all the people you know, how many of them would be thrilled to be as intuitive or as psychic as you are?

And, of all the people you know, how many of them would be ecstatic to know what the outcome of their latest stock-buying transaction will be?

Or, thinking about all of the people you know, would most of them marvel to feel or see and understand their Spirit Guide's instructions? (A Spirit Guide is the soul of a person who has agreed to guide, help, and protect you throughout periods during your life or your entire lifetime. With such a monumental task, you might want to get more familiar with your Spirit Guide and ask them their name.)

Would most of the people you know get excited to have the gift that enables them to see into the future, which would allow them to make the right decision?

Of course, they would! You could wager your last dollar that they would give everything they owned to be as psychic/sensitive/intuitive as you are, and that they would consider this gift a wondrous blessing, not a curse.

Being psychic is not a new thing. So, of all the people you know, the majority of them probably think you are unique and blessed! You can see the future so you know what to do, where to go, what to buy, and when to stay home. All of that really is wonderful!

What all or most of these people do not know is the upset you go through when you see a dark yet transparent figure, or a wisp of something out of the corner of your eye, or hear something said when no one else is around, or receive pictures in your mind. They cannot understand when you are going through the emotional turmoil you go through because you are picking up on or feeling someone else's emotions. Picking up these emotions can make you feel like an emotional sponge!

As I said, being psychic is not a new thing—there have been psychic/sensitive/intuitive people around for eons! They have been called sages, sorcerers, mystics, great teachers, and amazing healers. These people have safeguarded their mystical wisdom and were/are accomplished at using their supernatural gifts—or what appears to be supernatural, but were/are instead, in part, the use of herbs, intuition, the moon's phases, the power of forgiveness, and their own psychic gift. Of course, there were/are also witches and wizards who were/are amazing but feared and, most assuredly, envied for their limitless knowledge and uncanny power.

If you have noticed over the past few years more television programs have been devoted to the spiritual side of life—i.e., psychics, mediums or sensitive people who convey messages from the dead to the living—reincarnation and the proof of past lives, past-life regressions, ghost sightings, visitations by souls or spirits, and the mysterious afterlife. Because of the more recent attention focused on the spiritual side of life, it has become easier to talk about having the psychic gift and to learn about it.

By now, you are perhaps a bit more at ease with having the psychic gift. And you have acknowledged that you do see, feel or sense, and hear instruction, warnings, assistance, advice, inspiration, support, and/or spiritual insight from your Guardian Angels, Spirit Guide, and through your "hotline." We are now back to the second very important question I brought up earlier in this chapter, "How do you handle or manage this gift so it does not control you?"

First, accept that you have the psychic gift. Accept it, honor it, and be grateful for it. Having these three attitudes will make being blessed with this gift easier for you.

Accepting it puts you at ease, honoring it is better than fighting it, and being grateful for it can open the doors and bring you the help you need.

Second, the shadows of people you see out of the corner of your eye, seeing dark yet transparent people, hearing voices, and/or receiving pictures in your mind are some of the ways your psychic gift has been making itself known to you. The images or hearing what you did may have been frightening, but your psychic self certainly got your attention!

Third, practice the Shutting Down techniques in Part 3, Chapter 7. When you shut down your psychic gift, you are in control of what you are seeing, feeling, and/or hearing, which would be little or nothing when you are shut down.

Fourth, if and when you are ready, practice the Opening Up techniques in Chapter 8. When you open up your psychic gift, you are in control of *you* and your emotional self—not what comes in for you to see, feel or sense, hear, and/or become aware of psychically.

You become an observer and stop being an emotional sponge.

I will never forget the day I finally got a good strong handle on shutting down and then opening up. I felt like I had wings on my feet. I was as light as air because I had closed off or shut down all outside emotions that didn't belong to me. I was clean—so extremely clean and peaceful!

The shutting down techniques that gave me so much self-control and peace are listed in the "Shutting Down" chapter, but I want to share here with you the two techniques I often use.

One technique is to cover your forehead. This is the area known as the "third eye" chakra—a spiritual energy center sometimes referred to as the "All Seeing Eye." The forehead area or the "All Seeing Eye" is the area where psychic/sensitive/intuitive people see pictures, visions, or prophecies, and hear various types of messages or guidance.

Another method for shutting down that I use is physically to take a step backward, forward, to the left or to the right. This technique quickly moves a person out of the energy being felt or sensed. I often suggest this particular technique to people who are beginning to learn to manage their psychic gift.

Fifth, ask for help, clarity, understanding, a mentor, or whatever it is you think you need. I wish I'd had someone to ask for help when I was young. Perhaps my earlier years would have been easier. On the other hand, I understand and know the pain and frustration you are and have been experiencing, and I am sympathetic toward you because I have suffered, too. Best of all, now you know you are not alone, imagining things, or going off the deep end.

Let me introduce my mentors to you and share how they helped me.

My first mentor was a Tea Leaf reader who I met when I was around twelve years old. Actually, I was just tagging along with someone who wanted a Tea Leaf reading. When my friend's reading was finished, the Tea Leaf reader took my hand, lovingly looked me in the eyes, and told me I was extremely psychic.

Well, you can imagine!

There was silence in the room, my heart was pounding and my hands started sweating! She continued to look at me, smiling the entire time, and told me that I would find my way. That was it—*I would find my way.*

This brief encounter may not seem like much to you, but to me, it was the best gift I could have received at the time. She gave me the gift of peace. Her words confirmed what I secretly knew when I was six or seven years old: *I was psychic, not crazy!* I *was* hearing what I was hearing and I *was* seeing and sensing what I was seeing and sensing.

Looking back now, I believe my friend suspected I was psychic and asked the Tea Leaf reader to confirm it, and, if her suspicions were correct, to give me some guidance. This wonderful woman confirmed I had the psychic gift. As I discovered early on, most people with the psychic gift suspect they have it, but pooh-pooh the idea, try to ignore it, or fear it even more.

All the way home, and for days after, I reminded myself of her wise words—*I would find my way*. Little did I know then that it would be sixteen years of struggling to find my way to my second mentor, Jacqueline.

Yes, years before I had checked with many of my family members, quietly and discretely, and no one in my family, on either side, showed the signs of having the gift. I thought there was no one who could help me. Then Jacqueline came into my life when I was twenty-eight years old.

Jacqueline, a psychic, took me under her wing. She knew the agony, confusion, and fear I was experiencing. She knew I thought I was different, not special.

I worked the most with Jacqueline, but there were a few other psychics who helped me along my way. Jacqueline was the one who helped me the most. She helped me understand the fine line between other people's emotions and thoughts, and my own. She helped me understand many of the pictures, signs, and messages I saw and heard.

One evening, Jacqueline and I met with another psychic who focused her attention on Jacqueline for nearly one hour. At the end of the hour, she turned to me and said that I was very similar to a black stallion or a thoroughbred: strong, powerful, and high-strung.

Yes, my head swelled at the picture in my mind of a beautiful, shiny, black stallion standing tall and proud in the sunlight, his long mane brushed smooth, and his front hoof pawing the dirt.

Just as quickly, this psychic said the exact same thing the Tea Leaf reader told me years ago: *I would find my way.* Nothing more, not how I would find it, or where I would find it, or what I would do with it when I did find my way. It was just simply put: *I would find my way.*

A special note is needed here. When you receive the same message two or three times from different avenues, you are being told something important, something bearing repeating. I would find my way, and yes, I eventually did find my way, but I had help, a lot of help.

All the other wonderful psychics I worked with taught me about this, that, and the other stuff of being psychic, and I am grateful to those patient, loving psychics for sharing their wisdom and knowledge with me. They could not teach me everything in such a short time frame of three years, but I got the basics, and everything else I have learned has come to me via other teachers and in the Universe's perfect time.

During the time I worked with Jacqueline and the other psychics, there were no books on the subject of having the psychic gift and how to manage it, let alone what to do with it. And believe me, I looked! Now there are, thanks to the more recent attention given to the spiritual side of life.

There is something else you should know. There is another part of this amazing psychic gift you should be aware of, because it, too, develops as you learn about and begin to manage your gift. It is your spiritual self, your spiritual beliefs and knowledge, your compassion for your fellow beings and the lessons they are learning, usually the hard way, and your love of self, that grows and expands as you learn about your psychic gift.

Along the line of the development of your spiritual self, you may want to keep your "hotline" with God or your intuition clean and welcomingly open because, as I mentioned, you can receive such wondrous wisdom through it . . . wisdom unavailable any other way.

Welcome those souls or entities of people who have died, because some of them have messages for you, and some of them are observers. They bring you information, wisdom, and guidance, or they are observing you in order to learn something. These messengers or observers have a pleasant presence and have come to you out of love for you. These messengers or observers may still be dark figures, soft and wispy figures, orbs of light, or appear as the friends or loved ones you knew in this life before they died. They know you are aware of them, they know you have the gift.

Being psychic is not for the fragile, but then again, as I mentioned, you chose to have the psychic gift because you and God had a tremendous amount of confidence in you and all of the spiritual wisdom you have gained through the eons and your extraordinary integrity of heart. Embrace your gift and honor it.

God gifted you, blessed you with the psychic gift, and it is your choice whether to use it or not. Even if you just want to learn how to shut down your psychic gift but keep your "hotline" open, you can do that, too.

Remember, it is possible to manage your psychic gift instead of allowing it to control you. For me, being psychic is truly a gift, an amazing, valuable, wonderful gift, and a gift I am grateful for.

Chapter 4
Some of My Experiences

As I have mentioned before in this book, I have been aware of my psychic gift since I was about six or seven years old and I learned to follow my intuition early in life. I thought it might be helpful and perhaps even enjoyable for you if I shared some of my psychic episodes with you because you have probably had similar experiences.

Clairvoyant: Images, Visions

One evening in March, I had a dream. In this dream I saw a red planet, which was the planet Mars. A few nights later I saw this same red planet turn into a beautiful red heart. The next day, while I was shuffling my deck of Tarot cards, I picked a card with a beautiful red heart on it! The message that the Tarot card gave me was that someone on the Other

Side wished he had told me more often that he loved me. What a beautiful message.

S everal years ago, when my husband and I had our house built in the foothills, we discovered we needed some type of outdoor watering system for our gardens because all of our water came from our well and there were restrictions on using house water for watering gardens. Well, when you have berry and vegetable gardens, the produce you are growing needs water. So, I asked my Source for help in creating a watering system.

Within a few days of asking for help, a friend called me. She had four 15-gallon water barrels I could have if I wanted them. Naturally, I went to get them because we could store about sixty gallons of water in those four barrels.

Shortly after that, a neighbor called me to ask me if I would like to have their 200-gallon water tank. Wow! Well naturally, I said yes.

Now all I needed was some type of an outside flooring arrangement to keep the tanks off the ground, clean, and in place. How would I do that?

While doing the dishes a few days later, I saw a picture in my mind's eye or my "third eye" chakra that showed the layout of our 200-gallon tank and four 15-gallon barrels sitting on a large board. A board thick enough to stabilize the tanks and hold the weight of the water and, just by coincidence, was in my garage.

Lo and behold, as always, I was instructed through my "hotline" or my intuition as to how to set up the watering system for our garden, and the Universe provided the containers and picture instructions!

"Where did the water come from?" you might ask. A man who also had vegetable gardens and enjoyed gardening as much as we did delivered enough water to fill the tank and barrels for a small fee. As an added bonus, this man and I exchanged gardening information, including what size of submersible pump to buy in order to get the water out of the barrels and tank and onto the veggies and berries!

Clairsentient: Feeling, Sensing

When you know something, you just know it. One spring, my computer went down. Most of us know how that feels and how terrifying it can be! Anyway, my computer went down: not a virus, nothing simple. The hard drive would need to be rebuilt and that would take time.

Getting the hard drive rebuilt was one thing, but knowing the second computer we were using was going to go down soon was petrifying! Did the second computer go down? Yes. Did the second computer go down before my computer was repaired? Yes. How did I know this horrific event would take place? I just knew it.

Another one of my "hotline" experiences, which you may find interesting, was my experience of not going to the Hot Therapy pool on a Wednesday. I usually went to the therapy pool on Thursdays. On this particular Tuesday, I thought about going to the pool the next day, but for some reason the idea did not feel right so I put the thought away.

I stayed with my regular schedule and went to the Hot Therapy pool on Thursday. While there, I talked with a woman who had gone to the pool the day before, on Wednesday.

She told me that something had gone wrong with the pool's regulators. She told me that the water in the pool on Wednesday had been very cold and I should be glad that I had not gone to the pool that day. So, the "not right" feeling about going to the pool on Wednesday was my "hotline" or my intuition telling me it was not right to go on Wednesday, and on Thursday I found out why.

Clairaudient: Hearing

The following experience had a profound effect on my life and perhaps even saved it.

I was feeling fine but went to the doctor, a new doctor for me, for just a general checkup. After the exam, I followed him into his office. While walking down the hall, I heard in my head the word "butcher!" Immediately after I heard that, the hallway became black and very narrow with little air in it.

Before we entered his office, I heard the word again: "butcher." I could not wait to leave his office and admittedly, I had trouble focusing on what he was saying.

You might have run out of the building at this point, but for some reason I stayed.

He proceeded to tell me that should they find 'such and such,' they would do laser surgery, or if they found 'this and that,' they would perform minor surgery, or if they discovered the worst-case scenario, they would perform major surgery. He would not know until the test results came back. His office would call me in a few days and inform me of the results.

Well, as I said, I was feeling fine when I went to the doctor, had no symptoms of anything being wrong. And the test results? They were negative, of course. "Do you want to schedule more tests?" his receptionist asked me over the phone.

You know, I got off the phone as fast as I possibly could without being rude. Even now, when I think of him or see his face, I still hear the word "butcher." I am grateful I acted on my intuition and that my Spirit Guide and my Guardian Angels were protecting me.

Along this same line, a woman I know went to her doctor. In the waiting room she heard a whisper, and the whisper simply said, "It is a lie." After her examination, her test results came in. The doctor told her she had cancer. She was furious, demanded that the tests be run again, and told him, in no uncertain terms, that the first set of test results were wrong. He obliged and, lo and behold, the second sets of tests were negative. She, too, possesses the gift of being psychic.

Chapter 5
The Other Realm

W hat is the Other Realm, a.k.a., the Other Side or the Spirit World, that psychics and mediums talk about and that psychic/ sensitive/intuitive people feel so close to them?

It is a space inside, outside, and all around our three dimensional space, where the souls of the deceased live. Yes, you read it right, the Other Side is all around us, which is why sometimes you will see a bit of something dark out of the corner of your eye, a shadow of something moving in the corner, a quick breeze across your arm, or you suddenly get the shivers that stop just as quickly. These occurrences are some of the ways the souls or spirits on the Other Side extend us some type of greeting and either pass through or stay and share our three dimensional space.

Because this space is all around us, it can become a shared space with the living—for example, the hallway in your home. If you focus your attention on that hallway space, someone you know, but who has died, might be looking back at you and trying to communicate with you or give you some type of greeting. Or someone you do not know, but who has died, might be trying to give you a message. This explanation is not meant to frighten you, but to simply explain what the Other Realm, the Other Side, or the Spirit World is.

This space is not level with the ground we walk on and can be one foot, three feet, twelve feet or more above the ground. Just beneath that space where souls or spirits appear is a delicate, white cloud or vapor-like substance or mist that separates our three dimensional world and the Other Side.

From the many stories I have heard over the years from my mentors, teachers, other psychics and mediums, and from my own experiences talking with souls or spirits on the Other Side who come to visit— our deceased loved ones, acquaintances, and anyone else who passes over or dies has a life of sorts on the Other Side for a period of time.

During this life of sorts their time is spent learning new skills, perfecting talents, finishing lessons, exploring their environment, and helping the living until they decide to come back or reincarnate into this three dimensional world or space.

If you think about it, life after death is logical and environmentally friendly. Wouldn't it be a tremendous waste of joy, love, and learned experiences to live one life and then sit on a cloud, strumming a harp for all of eternity?

When I say, "helping the living," I mean that a deceased person's soul or spirit will come into our area, (for example the "hallway") to give you, me or anyone else help or direction via pictures or words of guidance, encouragement, comfort, or even a warning. This is when you, the psychic/sensitive/intuitive person that you are, will sense, feel, see, and/or perhaps hear this deceased person trying to communicate with you.

Here are a few of my experiences of communication with souls or spirits on the Other Side. I share them with you because chances are very good that you have had similar experiences and were frightened or thought you might be losing your mind or imagining things!

Many, many years ago, the soul of someone very dear to me who had just died the day before, came in to give me a message of comfort. At the time, I had fifteen plants in one corner of a room. It was a beautiful area filled with a small variety of different, healthy plants, and very peaceful.

This person's soul came in as a small, bright white orb of energy and simply nestled himself amongst the plants. The light would radiate brightly, become dim, and then grow bright again. Yes, I knew immediately that it was the soul of this very dear-to-me person. Sometime during his energy flickering, he sent to my intuitive self the message that he was OK and very happy!

Another example of my communication experiences with souls on the Other Side also took place many, many years ago and it, too, involved the death of someone very, very dear to me. This most beloved woman had died three days earlier. I had received no contact from her at all, and frankly, I was a bit upset that she had not yet come through to me.

She must have heard me, because that night we met in my dream. We met each other in a garden at the end of a cemetery I know, but not where she had been buried. In the midst of this garden are a few concrete walkways with very tall, pillar-like white columns at the walkways' centers and the corner edges. Covering the columns and the trellises are beautiful Trumpet Vine plants and other plants that vine and flower.

I walked up the steps to the concrete walkway where she greeted me. She wore a pale blue, very soft gown, and she looked healthy and rested.

Her message to me was not of comfort, but was one that would tell me, emphatically, that she was who she appeared to be and that she was all right. She looked at me and said, "This is not what it was cracked up to be!" I knew then she was who she appeared to be because she still had her particular sense of humor. I also knew what she meant when she said that Heaven was not what it was cracked up to be.

Her idea of Heaven was Angels singing, sitting on clouds, music playing, and peacefulness. For her, Heaven was this way when she first crossed over from her earthly life, because Heaven or the afterlife is what we believe it will be when we arrive . . . and then we get adjusted into our new surroundings or home. This is what happened to her and also what she meant when she told me it—Heaven—was not what it was cracked up to be. She did not expect to work or review her life. She expected to sit on a cloud and listen to Angels sing.

After she crossed over she rested for a time, but now she was being required by the upper echelon entities in the afterlife to review her life: how it was spent, the joy she had created, the pain she had inflicted on others, and the valuable lessons she had learned. After her review, she and some of the upper level entities would decide if it would be beneficial to her soul or spirit to come back or reincarnate in order to learn more lessons, fulfill desires, be of service, or experience something she wanted to learn.

From the many stories I have heard over the years, and from my own experiences when souls or spirits on the Other Side come to visit, they say or do something they did in life in order for us to recognize them. Next, the soul or spirit communicates to us, their loved ones, that they are OK. It seems as if many, many people want to know if their loved ones who have passed over or died are all right and what happens up or over there.

I have also learned from souls or spirits on the Other Side that the majority of them experienced Heaven or their entrance into the Other Realm as they had believed it would be—golden gates, Angels singing, etc. After their entrance, the souls or spirits rested for a while and then had a life review session followed by some sort of action, i.e., letting their loved ones know they were OK.

Because this chapter is about the Other Realm, a.k.a., the Other Side and the Spirit World, I would like to share with you this third true story. It illustrates how some souls or spirits on the Other Side or in the Spirit World learn from the living.

I was recovering from major knee surgery. From one week before the surgery to approximately one month after, I felt I was being watched—not all the time and oddly enough in only one area of my home, my bedroom!

Since I was approximately six or seven years old, I have had the feeling of being watched, and I was. And you, too, have probably felt as if you are being watched—not in a threatening way but, nevertheless, being watched.

As I said, since I was very young I felt I was being watched, and I was. I was being watched over and protected by my Spirit Guide and my Guardian Angels.

We are always watched over and protected by our Spirit Guide and by Guardian Angels, but this time it was a different feeling of being watched—one of actually being watched by souls or spirits I did not know and who did not guide or counsel.

Since I was busy recovering and rehabilitating my knee, I did not notice that I had received no communication from whoever was watching me during this five-week time-period. When I did realize it, I simply closed my eyes and focused my attention on the space in my bedroom being occupied by these souls or spirits.

As it turned out, there were three and sometimes four souls or spirits there. Only their heads and shoulders were visible and they appeared to be young, perhaps late teens or early twenties. They were grouped together above my closet but close to one corner of the room.

I must admit that I was a little startled to see this many souls. I asked them what they wanted and their response was crystal-clear and very surprising. One of them replied that they were learning from me! This response was shocking and set me back on my heels as the saying goes. When I regained my composure, I asked them what they were learning from me. Their answer: patience and perseverance.

As I learned, it took a lot of patience—two and one-half years to be exact—for the complete healing of bones, muscles, ligaments, and the like. It also took a tremendous amount of perseverance to rehabilitate my knee with exercises, maneuver around with a walker and then crutches, learn not to apply the car brakes with my healing leg, and everything else involved with a long recovery!

That was my first experience of souls or spirits coming around me to learn something they needed or wanted to learn from me. Since my knee surgery of more than thirty years ago, I have had other souls or spirits stay for a time to watch and learn whatever it is they have chosen to learn from me.

Perhaps sometime when you feel you are being watched, you probably are. And, in the watching of you, a soul or spirit is learning something he/she wants or needs to learn, something he/she is unable to learn in the space we call the Other Side or the Spirit World.

On the lighter side of being visited by souls or spirits—several times over the course of a one-month timeframe, after my husband and I adopted a kitten, two souls of children came in to play with Buddy, our kitten. How do I know that? Well, of course, I saw them, and so did Buddy.

Buddy would look up to one certain spot in our living room, very close to the high ceiling. He would stare at this spot for a moment or two and then begin to run around, jump in the air, and simply play.

If you have a cat or a dog, watch him/her. Does your pet stare at a particular spot and then play or wander off, fulfilled by the attention he/she just received? Does your pet ignore you or your command and then run off? Chances are very good your pet is visiting or playing with someone from the Other Side.

Has your salt or peppershaker moved, even a fraction of an inch from where you were positive you put it? Or your keys moved a few inches to the left or right of where you put them? Or the pen you are sure you clicked off is now clicked on?

Look around the salt or peppershaker, your keys or your pen. Do you see the delicate, white cloud or vapor-like substance or mist that sometimes accompanies a soul or spirit when they come to visit us from the Other Side?

It is not your imagination. You have been visited by a soul or spirit of someone from the Other Realm, the Other Side or the Spirit World. Why? This soul or spirit is simply letting you know that he/she is around and is all right, and knows you are psychic/sensitive/intuitive enough to acknowledge and greet him/her. Perhaps this soul has a message for you, or perhaps you know this soul and he/she wants you to know that he/she is all right. Or perhaps this soul has chosen to learn something from you.

The Other Realm or the Other Side is all around us. It is where the souls or spirits of our loved ones live. It is a space where we can meet them for a period of time to learn and share and be touched by pure love.

Part 3

The Techniques

**For the young, teenagers, and the not so young:
ages eight to eighty**

Chapter 6
The Chakras

I ncluded here is a chapter on the chakras or the seven areas of energy located inside the Spiritual body that lives inside the human body of each person. I have included this chapter in order for you to familiarize yourself with this area of the psychic gift because you, the psychic/sensitive/intuitive person that you are, have and do see, sense, and/or feel other people's emotions and/or thoughts. You may also hear voices and/or words in your chakra centers. You receive "gut instincts" about people, situations, and experiences in some of these energy centers as well.

If at some point in time you choose to use your psychic gift to help other people via psychic readings, you would be using your chakra system to help you read a person as well as read that person's energy or chakra system.

"Chakra" is the Sanskrit word for wheel or disk. The chakras are seven energy centers or wheels or disks that live within the Spiritual body that lives within the physical body. They are invisible. They are a person's life force and vitality, and are essential to good health.

The flow of energy from one chakra to the next is called the "Kundalini Flow" or "Prana" and starts at the base of the spine, aligns with it, and travels up through the body to the top or the crown of the head.

Each chakra or energy center swirls with colored energy that corresponds to the seven colors in the rainbow. Each is seen or felt as the predominant color in someone's aura, such as self-confident yellow. And each is linked to various emotions, and is associated with the nerve centers, organs, and the glandular system. Five of the seven chakras are linked with the type of psychic gift you have: clairsentience or feeling and sensing; clairaudience or hearing; and/or clairvoyance or seeing visions or images.

As I mentioned, it is important for you to know about the chakras because you see, sense, or feel, and/or hear energy or other people's emotions and/or thoughts in your chakra centers. For example, you feel a person's anxiety or confidence in your third or Solar Plexus chakra. You feel love for or from someone in your Heart chakra. And you would see a coming event in your sixth, Brow or the "third eye" chakra.

The "chakras of matter" or the second, third, and fourth chakras, physically inform you if someone is angry, afraid, or nervous, or if you have been told a lie. For example, if you have been told a fib, your "gut instinct" is disbelief—your head may pull back a little, your tummy may tighten, a slimy feeling may come over you, or you may see in your mind's eye a red warning light. Seeing the red warning light in your mind's eye is the "third eye" chakra, a spiritual energy center. If you are around another person who is angry, a picture of red-hot flames may come into your mind, or you may feel heat in your Solar Plexus area also referred to as the "feeling the truth" chakra.

Energy, be it positive or negative, travels up and down your spine, around your body, from me to you and from you to me, through walls and floors and into the galaxy and beyond.

When you think about thoughts and emotions traveling through space, remember this: our emotions and our thoughts are energy and they become real things.

For example, if you put out into space or affirm (a positive statement made to the self) that you are lovable, other people begin to see and sense you as being a lovable, loving person.

Likewise, if you are constantly depressed, depressing energy surrounds you and it draws or attracts people, experiences, and situations that increase your depression.

Another example might be that you have been affirming that you have changed jobs, moved into a more relaxed work environment with helpful, supportive, and pleasant co-workers, have a supportive and approachable employer, and received an increase in wages.

By continually affirming this positive desire, you created positive energy, the energy needed to move you into this new job. The positive energy you created went through space to the person who chose to hire you. When you interviewed for the job, it was not so much what your resume read or what you said in the interview. It was the energy your new employer felt from you, which was the same energy you sent out that he/she felt or sensed. In other words, your energy and your new employer's energy resonated and brought the two of you together.

Energy travels! And, because you have the psychic gift, you see, feel, or sense, and/or hear it. Another example might be that you see or sense a person's red-orange aura or vibrating light because he/she is very fearful of losing his/her job. The red energy comes from the first or Root chakra, an area dealing with earthly matters (finances) and the orange energy comes from the second or Navel chakra or the raw emotion of fear in this example.

You may see or sense someone's yellow aura because of his/her high level of self-confidence. The yellow energy comes from the third or Solar Plexus chakra.

We all work with different chakras at different times in our life, which means your aura would change colors or the colors of the chakras you are working with would blend. For example, someone might see or sense the color of lavender around you if you are working with the sixth, Brow or "third eye" chakra— its color is purple—and the seventh, Crown or "thousand-petal lotus" chakra—its color is white. Together, purple and white make lavender, which is why someone may sense the color lavender around you.

The Chakras

The "chakras of matter" or physical concerns are the first three chakras after the first or Root chakra. The "chakras of matter" are the Navel, the Solar Plexus, and the Heart chakras. These energy centers are connected with earthly matters: food, shelter, fear, change, depression, personal power, procreating, the desire to be stable or have stability, and love.

The Heart chakra is the center of the seven chakras—where the "chakras of matter" and the three spiritual centers meet.

The three spiritual centers are the fifth or Throat or "speaking and hearing" chakra, the sixth or the "third eye" chakra, and the seventh or the Crown chakra also known as the "thousand-petal lotus."

THE FIRST, Root or the Base chakra is red in color, is located at the base of the spine, and is associated with the adrenal gland. It is where the beginning of spiritual enlightenment occurs. If there were one sentence to describe the Root chakra it would be: trust the Universe to provide all you need, such as food and shelter. This area deals with overcoming insecurities concerning not enough food or money, inadequate shelter, needing physical or financial security, stability in life, and releasing fear. It is also associated with "fight or flight" energy or self-protection.

THE SECOND, Navel or the "creativity and sexual" chakra is orange in color, is located below the navel, and is associated with the reproductive system. This is the area of creativity of all types, including procreating or having children, giving and receiving, and raw emotions such as fear or anger. This is also the area associated with depression and the fear of change. The clairsentient or feeling and sensing psychic gift is associated with this chakra.

THE THIRD or Solar Plexus chakra is yellow in color, is located around the navel, and is associated with digestion, metabolism, the liver, spleen, stomach, and pancreas. It is a person's personal power area, self-confidence, self-esteem, and decisiveness. It is referred to as the seat of knowingness or *feeling the truth*. This is where a psychic/sensitive/intuitive person will feel or sense other people's emotions, being told a lie, or receive a "gut instinct" to do or not do something. The clairsentient or feeling and sensing psychic gift is associated with this chakra.

THE FOURTH or Heart chakra is green in color, is located in the center of the chest, and is associated with the heart, lungs, blood circulation, thymus gland, and the lymphatic system. If there were four words to describe the Heart chakra, they would be "love," "compassion," and, of course, "unconditional love." As we all know, one of the most incredible feelings there is is the feeling of love from or for someone. The clairsentient or feeling and sensing psychic gift is associated with this chakra.

THE FIFTH, Throat or "speaking and hearing" chakra is blue in color, is located in the throat area, and is associated with the thyroid gland. This chakra is the area of a person's expertise at speaking in the higher or spiritual manner, which is speaking with kindness, love, and compassion, and sharing the highest wisdom and knowledge possessed. It is also the "hearing" chakra, which requires listening with full attention to both the speaker and intuition. The clairaudient or hearing psychic gift is associated with this chakra.

THE SIXTH, Brow or "third eye" chakra is purple or indigo in color, is located between the eyebrows, and is associated with vision, the left (receiving) eye, the ears, and the pituitary gland. If it could be seen, intuition or the "hotline" tube lives here. The clairvoyant or seeing visions or images psychic gift is associated with this chakra.

THE SEVENTH, Crown or the "thousand-petal lotus" chakra is white or violet in color, is located at the top of the head, and is associated with the right (sending and seeing ahead or seeing into the future) eye, spiritual enlightenment and spiritual connection to our higher self, the divine, and all of life. In this chakra, a person is no longer concerned about self, personal goals, or ego. Instead, a person is spending time serving humanity in some fashion, giving unconditional love, and flowing with and being a positive part of the Universe.

As I mentioned, it is important for you to know about the chakras because you, the psychic/ sensitive/intuitive person that you are, see, sense, or feel, and/or hear other people's emotions and/or thoughts or feel their energy in your chakra centers. What you see, sense, or feel, and/or hear is the energy of different chakra lessons being learned or issues being dealt with by other people.

For example, you may see, sense, or feel fear or uneasiness in your second, Navel or "creativity and sexual" chakra because the person you are speaking with is fearful for some reason.

Or your stomach may start churning because the person you are with has an upset stomach (third or Solar Plexus chakra). He/she is indecisive about an important matter and the indecisiveness is "hard to stomach."

Because the issues or lessons belong to another person, you can simply let go of their energy or shut down your own receptive energy. Remember: if you choose to shut down your energy, be assured you will be safe. Your Root chakra ("fight or flight" warning energy) and your intuition or your "third eye" chakra (guidance) will remain open to protect and guide you.

Chapter 7
Shutting Down

*Y*ou can shut down, turn off, or close down other people's distractions: anxieties, nervousness, depression, anger, and the other emotions that feel like an assault upon your being. And for clarity's sake, when you shut down, you are temporarily shutting down or closing off your chakra system (except the Root and "third eye" chakras) and are shielding your Spiritual and emotional bodies. It simply takes practice.

You do need to learn how to shut down these distractions—because there are events you need to attend, get-togethers you would like to participate in, co-workers you need to interact with, people you need to talk to, and perhaps a group or two you would like to join as a member. And you will not enjoy yourself doing any of the above if you are feeling assaulted by outside distractions such as Jack's anxiety or Mary's depression.

When I say, "shut down the distractions," I mean shutting down or closing the door and not owning or being another person's emotion, such as angry or depressed. Shutting down does not mean you ignore someone's pain or suffering; you simply are aware that that emotion belongs to him/her and not to you.

Yes, you can share with Mary that you are aware of her sorrow and perhaps inquire if there is anything you can do to help. She may simply need someone to talk to about her experience. And, yes, you can acknowledge to Jack that you are aware of his anxiety and perhaps ask him why he is anxious. Perhaps you know a good joke that would help calm him.

You want to be aware of the distractions, not own them, or, in other words, become anxious because you are picking up Jack's anxiety or suddenly become full of sorrow because you are picking up or feeling or sensing Mary's depression.

You can shut down, turn off, or close down other people's emotions and/or thoughts, and you can shut down those other distractions, too. The distractions created from those dark and mysterious figures lurking in the corner, the soft and wispy figures you see out of the corner of your eye, or those little bright, white orbs of light you see every now and then, and the muffled voices you sometimes hear.

You can shut down, turn off, or close down the above distractions and the emotions or thoughts of other people but you cannot shut down or turn off your "hotline" (intuition) or your Root chakra. These two areas remain open, which they need to be in order to guide you, give you a warning, inspire you, or protect you.

And they need to be *on* to protect you, such as when you are crossing the street or driving your car or are in unfamiliar territory. Suffice it to say, with the exception of your "hotline" and Root chakra, you can shut down, turn off, or close down, and then cleanse yourself of the distractions in order to enjoy life.

Have you heard the saying: "thoughts are things"— this is true. Whatever you think a lot about is created or becomes real. You have noticed this phenomena happening in your life, I am sure. I bring this up because some of the shutting down techniques are done in your mind or successfully accomplished by your thinking. Other shutting down procedures will be performed physically.

The power of your mind is awesome. Remember that when you start practicing the shutting down techniques listed. Be certain to make each image in your mind as real looking as you possibly can.

Remember, also, that you will need to practice these techniques repeatedly when you feel the onslaught of emotions or begin to get distracted, especially when you are in the company of other people.

As you practice, you will find that, for you, certain techniques will work better than others will. Use those until you have mastered them and can perform them in the blink of an eye, so that when you do become uncomfortable in some situation you can quickly regain control of you. Become an observer instead of an emotional sponge—ignore the distractions and enjoy whom you are with and where you are.

Shutting Down the Chakras in Your Mind

*E*ven though you cannot shut down your Root or "hotline" (intuition) chakras, include them in the shutting down exercises to maintain a continuous flow of energy.

#1. Imagine in your mind each chakra or energy center. Each one has a dark brown wooden door in front of it. See your hand reaching for the doorknob and closing the door. Start at the top of your head or the Crown chakra and continue down to the first or the Root chakra closing each door as you move down.

#2. Imagine in your mind a brightly colored shower curtain on the window of each chakra or energy center.

The curtains are open. See your hands quickly pulling the shower curtain closed on each window or chakra as you move from the top of your head to the base of your spine.

#3. Imagine in your mind a tie-down lid above each chakra. Quickly tie the lid on each energy center.

Shutting Distractions Off in Your Mind

#1. Imagine in your mind a big light switch. Reach up and turn this switch to the "off" position. By turning the switch to the "off" position, you have turned off the distractions. This allows you to focus on a person or the experience you choose.

#2. In your mind, see yourself inside a brick box with a concrete floor. Feel the roughness of the brick and the concrete. Because you have surrounded yourself with a brick box and are standing on a concrete floor, you cannot feel other people's emotions or receive their thoughts.

#3. In your mind, imagine yourself surrounded by a beautiful yellow, lightweight drape or curtain. This drape is protective, is the color of happiness, and shields you from receiving other people's emotions and/or thoughts.

#4. In your mind, imagine yourself surrounded by a very thick, clear shield. It is so thick other people's emotions and/or thoughts simply bounce off the shield.

#5. Immediately refocus your attention onto something that brings you pleasure, such as reading a book. When your attention is on something pleasurable, other people's negative emotions cannot come through.

#6. See yourself vacuuming you. Imagine all the negative emotions and/or thoughts being sucked into the vacuum cleaner wand, and then hear them whirling around in the canister.

#7. If it feels like someone, a soul or spirit from the Other Side or the Other Realm is making every effort to have your attention, you can tell that soul or spirit to leave you alone. You can tell that soul or spirit you do not have time for him/her right now and to, please, leave you alone. Trust me . . . he/she will dissolve away. A side note here: if this soul or spirit has a specific message for you or a warning or something very important you need to know, he/she will continue to try to give you that message.

#8. Psychic Indigestion. This uncomfortable digestive disorder is caused by trying to learn too much at once without allowing your system time to digest what you have learned and/or put into practice what you have learned. It is also caused from being around too much energy and not protecting yourself or shutting down.

This technique helps eliminate Psychic Indigestion. Imagine putting your feet under the dryer vent and feeling the warm air blowing on them. The heat from this imaginary dryer vent will help purify your system and cleanse away negative energy.

Shutting Distractions Off Physically

There are techniques you can perform that will physically stop the incoming emotional assault you feel—the assault being other people's negative emotions and/or thoughts or a soul or spirit wanting your attention.

#1. Lift and then cross your left ankle over your right foot. The left side is the receiving side or where energy comes in. By lifting your left foot out of the negative energy field, you break the circuit of receiving.

#2. Lift and then cross your left leg over your right knee. Just as in #1, you are breaking the circuit of receiving.

#3. Take your left hand, and with palm down, position your hand over your bellybutton. If possible, cover your left hand with your right hand, palm down. The bellybutton area is in front of the adrenal gland or the "fight or flight" gland or self-protection gland. And you probably do feel as if you want to take flight if you are in uncomfortable energy, such as someone releasing his/her anger. This is also the area of the third chakra where a person's personal power resides. Covering the bellybutton protects your personal power from attack or from being taken away or weakened by negative energy.

#4. Similar to #3, use a small pillow to cover your bellybutton area.

#5. Close your left hand by placing your fingers pointing into the palm of the left hand. Cover the left hand with the right hand, the right hand fingers going over the back of the left hand toward the left hand wrist.

#6. Cover your forehead. This is the area known as the "third eye" chakra, a.k.a., the "All Seeing Eye." This is the area where psychic/sensitive/intuitive people see pictures, visions, or prophecies, and hear voices or words of inspiration or wisdom. Covering your forehead allows you take a break, so to speak, from receiving. Remember: you cannot close down, turn off, or shut down your intuition or "hotline."

#7. Close your eyes and massage the area above your eyebrows. This will look like you are simply resting your eyes and massaging your brow, but you are temporarily closing down the reception of your "third eye" chakra as in #6. And it feels good, too!

#8. Take a step backward, forward, to the left or the right. This will physically remove you from the energy in that particular area.

#9. Using a soft breath, exhale deeply out between your lips. This will blow the energy away from you. You can turn your head back and forth to blow away the emotions, thoughts, or negative energy you do not want in your immediate space.

#10. Hold your left hand up or your left arm out in front of you in the "stop" position. This will stop the energy coming toward you.

#11. Hold your left hand over your heart to protect your Heart chakra from receiving negative energy.

#12. Place your hands in front of you and sweep away the energy.

#13. Keep your fingernails short. Your fingernails are receivers of energy. Keeping them short helps lessen the receipt of other people's energy.

Cleansing

Sometimes the bombardment of other people's emotions or of their thoughts, or even the distractions by visiting souls or spirits of the dead can make a psychic/sensitive/intuitive person feel soiled. When this happens to you, take some time to cleanse yourself.

The cleansing techniques in this section are performed in your awesomely powerful mind, with the exception of the shower cleansing procedures. They, too, can be done in your mind if taking a shower is not possible at the time.

#1. Go outside and walk around until you find a comfortable spot. Take a moment to stand still and then allow all of the emotions, thoughts or distractions you do not want to feel or know about to go down into the earth.

#2. Go outside and sit in a comfortable chair. Take a moment to breathe in deeply three times and exhale slowly three times. While breathing deeply, tell yourself gently and lovingly that you are clean and peaceful. Remain outside for a few more moments and enjoy the sunshine.

#3. Go into the nearest restroom and wash your hands. While you are washing your hands, breathe in deeply three times and out three times. In your mind, watch those uncomfortable emotions, thoughts, and/or distractions going down the drain.

#4. In your mind, imagine a huge piece of tape gently surrounding you, pulling off all the negative energy, and then imagine the tape jumping into the garbage dumpster.

#5. In your mind, see yourself standing on the conveyor belt at the car wash moving through the rinse, wash, and rinse cycles.

#6. Cleansing shower (a) - This technique can be executed while you are taking a shower or imagining in your mind that you are taking a shower. Get wet, soap up, scrub a dub dub, and rinse. Now envision yourself covered in a beautiful white gown or shirt and slacks. White is the symbol of purity.

#7. Cleansing shower (b) - Sprinkle one or two table-spoons of Epsom Salt under your feet while you are taking a shower. The Epsom Salt will help purge the body of negative energy picked up during the day.

#8. Cleansing bath. Add one or two tablespoons of Epsom Salt to your bath water to help remove negative energy from the body.

#9. Feet Soaker. Soak your feet in comfortably hot water and Epsom Salt. As in #7 and #8, the salt will help cleanse the body of negative energy.

#10. As mentioned in the "Shutting Distractions Off in Your Mind" section, Psychic Indigestion comes from trying to learn too much at once without allowing your system time to digest what you have learned and/or put what you have learned into practice. It is also caused from being around too much energy and not protecting yourself or shutting down. If you have a case of Psychic Indigestion, try this exercise. Gently rock yourself in a rocking chair or rock from side to side on your bed.

With practice, practice, and more practice, using the techniques listed in this section you can shut down or close off distractions and feeling or sensing other people's anxieties, nervousness, anger, and the other emotions that feel uncomfortable, even sickening, and that deplete your energy or feel like an assault upon your being. With practice, you will be able to shut down or close off in the blink of an eye.

Also with practice, you can quickly clean your "hotline" of intuition. As I mentioned in, "The Gift of Being Psychic" chapter, your intuition is your guidance center, the area where you receive instruction, inspiration, wisdom, and warnings.

From your guidance center, usually through that unmistakable "wee small voice" you hear, comes instruction or warnings, such as do not drive your usual route, avoid so-and-so today, or do not sign that contract.

If you followed the instruction or warning, you would have avoided being stuck in traffic caused by a car accident or being involved in one yourself. Or avoided so-and-so because she was in such a horrible mood that no one wanted to be around her. Or not signed the contract that was written in such a way that the particular house you were thinking about renting or purchasing would have cost you more money.

However, if you misunderstood or ignored the instruction or warning you received, you might have been stuck in traffic or been involved in a car accident, been brought to tears or the boiling point by so-and-so's horrible mood, or bought a very expensive house. All good reasons to keep your "hotline" clean!

Also, through your "hotline" of intuition or guidance center come words and pictures of inspiration or ideas about creating things of beauty, such as a piece of sculpture that looks like chiffon instead of marble, or making something useable and beneficial, such as the light bulb or the wheel.

Another reason to keep your "hotline" of intuition or guidance center clean is the words of wisdom it brings—wisdom that passes all understanding. Your "hotline" presents you with the understanding of why something happened the way it did or why so-and-so is in your life. It can direct you on which car to buy, when to buy a house, or when to stay off the highway. Your intuition will give you guidance and instruction on how to make your dream career a reality. It will even inform you of what your purpose in life is.

To receive such wisdom clearly, keep the connection between you and your "hotline" clean! Similar to the other cleansing techniques in this chapter do these cleansings in your mind and once a day or more often if you have been around negative energy.

#1. Remember the "rabbit ear" antenna that once sat on top of the television that you, your parents or grandparents owned? Imagine it securely attached to the top of your head. Take a soft, soap-soaked cloth and go over every inch of it. Take another soft, damp cloth and go over the antenna wiping away the soap and negativity.

#2. Clean your forehead ("third eye" chakra) with some cool water and then polish it until it sparkles.

If you need to, make a promise to yourself to listen to your intuition for fifteen minutes every day and whenever it needs to give you a warning. Get into the habit of meditating or, if nothing else, sitting still with your eyes closed for ten to fifteen minutes a day. You will find it is time well spent.

So for now, practice shutting off or closing down other people's emotions and the distractions caused by the souls or spirits of those who have passed over (died). And believe that you can create a safe haven for yourself using your mind and simple techniques.

Chapter 8
Staying Centered

In Chapter 7 "Shutting Down," in the "Shutting Distractions Off in Your Mind" section, we talked about your focus—"#5. Immediately refocus your attention onto something that brings you pleasure." The best way to shut down and remain that way is to consistently be centered in you—"you" being your heart—in your creative endeavors or in some activity that brings you pleasure. Being centered in you does not mean being self-centered.

Being centered in you fills you with you and then puts a beautiful shield or bubble around you that keeps out other people's emotions and/or thoughts, and it keeps the dark and mysterious figures or the soft and wispy figures at bay. It also allows your "hotline" or your intuition easy access to you so you can clearly see, feel, or sense, and/or hear what you need to, such as the answer you have needed to complete a project you have been working on or what the next step is in order to get you where you want to go.

To illustrate what I mean when I say "stay centered in you," watch a cat at play.

The cat is completely focused on what he is playing with and is engaged in playing with it. He does not see the wall he is about to run into or the water on the floor from his water bowl that he spilled while playing with his toy.

He does not see the toy he sent rolling across the floor as he chased the ball of yarn and batted it around because he is playing. He is focused on the ball of yarn he is playing with. He is centered in self and he is happy.

Being happy is the keyword when it comes to being centered in self. The most beautiful, pleasant, and peaceful experience to have is to watch someone, or the cat, centered in self and happy.

A young woman I know designs and makes quilts in her free time. She loves making them. They are very time-consuming designs, and much of the work requires her complete attention. When she is working on a quilt, nothing irritates or frightens her. Not even the noise of chitchat distracts her from her center. She is at peace, very happy, and is so much in love with the quilt she is working on that her love is transferred into it, which a person can feel when the quilt is touched.

During her workday and at other times, she recalls the happiness and peacefulness she experiences while making quilts and infuses these two emotions into the task at hand. Her work requires tremendous focus and attention to important details. She is the supervisor of a team of five people. Not one of them has ever said that she loses her temper, is short with people or says a negative word about anyone. In fact, she is always pleasant to be around.

Another woman I know is an accountant. She is also a delight to watch because she, too, is happily centered in self. No amount of transposed numbers or out-of-balance columns can get her off center. She does not lose her temper, say a negative word about anyone, or use a condescending tone of voice while talking to her co-worker who made a mistake. She walks and sits in her center: straight and tall, no leaning to one side or the other, and no hunching over the calculator or the desk.

And a gardening companion of mine is also gifted at staying in her center, especially when she is gardening or cooking. I have watched her pull weeds for an hour at a time and not get discouraged at the shear number of the invasive plant life in the next row over or feel the temperature rising as noon approaches. She is just as pleasant to talk with at high noon as she was two hours earlier.

My friend's center is filled with love for her garden as she tends it, and pleasure as she thinks about how delicious those fresh beans will taste when she steams them and then adds some butter and fresh bacon to them.

These three women, and many other people, learned how to get and stay centered in self while being attentive to whatever they were doing, being comfortable in their skin, and infusing happiness, love, and contentment into the task at hand.

Infusing positive emotions is the key because they fill you up and then spill over beyond your shield or bubble and into your environment. And it certainly is much more pleasant to be centered in and radiating out a happy, peaceful you rather than a fearful, upset you.

Remember that being centered fills you with you and then puts a beautiful shield or bubble around you that keeps out other people's emotions and/or thoughts.

Chapter 9
Opening Up

Now that you have practiced and perfected shutting down your psychic gift, you can do the same with opening it up.

What is different now is that you are in control of you! You can be an observer of and acknowledge other people's emotions and/or thoughts instead of being an emotional sponge, and you can acknowledge and observe the souls and spirits of people who have passed over (died) instead of fearing them.

Two very important notes here: remember to shut down! If you remain open, you can easily tire out or drain yourself and that will make you more susceptible to emotional bombardment. Be open for a time to receive messages, feel, sense, or listen, and then shut down or close off.

The second important note: before opening up, take a few moments to double-check that you know yourself. There are some people who will try to manipulate a good person such as you.

Think about this example of manipulation. You are normally an energetic person who enjoys getting one project done and is enthusiastic about tackling the next job . . . *but* the person you have been working with is not.

Your co-worker is just the opposite of you. She prefers to socialize, make personal calls, and spend the time you work together complaining about this, that, and the other. In short, she prefers not to work and wishes you were more like her.

As time goes by, you begin to agonize over working with this person, and when you two do get together you are having trouble focusing on the job. Soon after, you find yourself creating excuses to put off working on this project that you used to be so excited and enthusiastic about.

If you know yourself, you will think it is odd that since you have been working with this one particular person you have lost your excitement for this project. And, because you really enjoy completing tasks, you will think it is out of the ordinary that you are creating excuses to not finish this one.

What happened? You know yourself, and you observed the energy changing; however, looking back, perhaps you should have taken some action sooner? Perhaps you should have shut down and observed? Perhaps asked for a different co-worker to help you finish the project? As I said, there are some people who will try to manipulate a good person such as you, which is why you need to know yourself.

The first step in opening up, *after* you double-check that you know yourself, is for you to protect you. This can be done several ways, and just as in shutting down, you will want to find and use the techniques that work the best for you.

Protection

#1. Ask the Good Lord, God, the Universe (or whomever you believe your source to be) to surround you with the protective white light of the Holy Spirit. Then, in your mind, see yourself surrounded in beautiful shimmering white light. This is a very nice way to start your day!

#2. In your mind, surround yourself with a clear shield or bubble. You can see out clearly, but distractions cannot get inside your shield or bubble.

#3. In your mind, see yourself wearing a raincoat finished in your favorite color.

Observe and Take Note

Now that you have your protection on, move forward into using your psychic gift. Acknowledge that dark yet transparent figure that has been lurking in the corner for ages and ask him his name and what he wants. Be an observer and listen to his answer. After he shares his name with you, his answer could be anything! It might be one word or he might give you a picture.

Those soft and wispy figures you have seen out of the corner of your eye? Follow the same procedure: greet them, ask for names, and ask if they want something. Do the same thing when those little bright white orbs of light come around you.

If you hear voices, listen to them. Does the voice of the departed soul or entity want you to do something? Immediately tune into your "gut instinct" area—the third or Solar Plexus chakra—to see how this area feels. Does it feel tight, uneasy, or calm? Reminder: this "gut instinct" area or "feeling the truth" chakra is the place in your physical body where you will feel or sense that something said or asked for is positive, informative, kind, or hurtful and negative.

Back to hearing voices and staying tuned into your "gut instinct" area. Does what the voices ask or say seem a good thing? Such as, "Tell Mom I'm OK," "Sorry that I could never finish the garage," or "I loved to read that book over and over again." *If* their words resonate with truth in your "gut instinct" area or the "feeling the truth" chakra, they are a positive entity or soul. *If* what they ask or say sends chills down your spine, tightens the muscles in your stomach, or makes you feel the slightest bit uneasy, *do not* indulge them, and forcefully tell them to leave.

Remember, you are in control of you, and you are an observer. The souls or spirits of those who have died come around you because they want to. They may have a loved-filled message for you or need to tell you something important. Perhaps you may know this soul or spirit who has come in to let you know he/she is all right or to simply check on you.

When it comes to opening up, each psychic person receives messages, pictures, and symbols. The more you use your gift, the easier it becomes to understand what you are being told through pictures and symbols. You may want to start a diary or notebook that contains the symbols and pictures you receive. The following describes what seem to be fairly common symbols and pictures among psychics.

Pictures and Symbols

Seeing the name of a month indicates some type of an event transpiring in or around that month.

Seeing a planet or cluster of planets, points to some type of celestial transit that will affect you, such as seeing the planet Venus. The planet Venus rules love, appreciation of the arts, and money. Seeing the planet Venus could indicate a new relationship forming.

Seeing money, paper bills or coins generally indicates money coming to you. Or if you see the face of someone you know included with the money, then money may be coming to or from him/her.

Seeing hearts indicates love and affection coming to you.

Seeing symbols of holidays and birthdays heralds a time when our loved ones who have passed over come to visit the living. It could also indicate some type of positive event transpiring around that time, such as a wedding or a new job.

Seeing suitcases indicates an opportunity for travel.

Seeing a telephone indicates the possibility of some form of higher communication.

Seeing boxes in the living room usually is a message that you or someone you know may be moving.

Seeing snow, snowflakes, or snowstorms represents the winter season; a time to slow down and reflect; an event or action on hold.

Physical Body

Be attentive to your body's reactions to what you feel or sense, the message received, or what you hear. For example, positive, love-filled messages, good news or the right decision made by you or someone else will make you feel more at ease and your tummy relax, and you will feel good about the message received or the decision made.

Negative energy, a lie or untruth, the wrong course of action, or the wrong decision will tighten your tummy or whole body, send shivers down your spine, and/or somehow make you feel uncomfortable.

Nervous or restless energy may give you a headache or upset stomach, or make you feel suddenly fatigued.

Notes

To open up or start off using your psychic gift will probably not make you immediately partake in ghost hunting, conjure up negative or unhappy entities, or jump into giving psychic readings.

You will probably start small, going to a get-together where you know some of the people who will be attending. You will most definitely ask for or put on your shield of protection, observe, and enjoy yourself. Be sure to give yourself a pat on the back for being and staying in control of you.

In your diary or notebook of pictures and symbols you may want to write down or make notes of how well you did, what and/or whom you observed, how delightful it was to enjoy other people instead of becoming an emotional sponge, and anything else that might help you in the future.

Use your psychic gift. Go to a restaurant or coffee shop. Without intruding into any person's private life or space, ask your gift if that person is happy or sad and what they do for a living, and then listen to and trust the answer.

Read or hear the ending score of the game *before* the game starts.

Walk through a cemetery and listen. What or who do you hear?

Hold a necklace or watch of someone you do not know. What do you sense, see, or hear about that person? Trust your answers.

Go to a garage sale, estate sale, or a second-hand shop. Pick up a book, a scarf, or a belt. What do you sense, see, or hear about its previous owner?

Trust your first impression, trust your first impression, and trust your first impression. It may come as a lightning-quick, crystal-clear picture or a "gut instinct." It may come as a positive or negative feeling or a soft voice whispering something important. Have confidence in and trust your first impression. Here is a story that shows why these two things are so important.

I remember meeting a man at a wedding many, many years ago. His handshake was the equivalent of holding cold, cooked spaghetti noodles—or, better put, it was wimpy and slimy. He was surrounded by blackness—not darkness, but blackness. And, when I looked into his face, he had no face! I had not ever experienced this type of a first impression, and let me tell you, it was frightening and certainly a very clear message or feeling telling me to stay away from him.

One year later, this man left the woman he had married. I was told that he had stolen as much of her money as he could throughout the year, and that he also used and abused her.

Seeing no face and seeing blackness were the signs or symbols indicating that he was trying to hide his true self—a thief and an abuser. And here is an interesting side note: a few of the other people at the wedding received a similar first impression to the one I received. Trust your first impression and have confidence in what you receive, because sooner or later, you will understand why you picked up or received what you did.

Practice each and every day. Trusting your first impression takes practice, so here is a helpful exercise. As you walk through your workplace, be aware of the first impression you receive regarding each of your co-workers. You may receive a psychic impression that Mary did not sleep well, Joe is cranky, or Barb is hungry. You can chat with them throughout the day to check how accurate your first impression was.

Here is another helpful exercise. Walk through a shopping mall and be aware of your first impression when you greet someone else walking alongside you. Trust your first impression and have confidence in what you receive.

Always thank and extend gratitude to God, the Good Lord, the Universe (or whomever you consider your source to be) for the pictures, symbols, and/or messages you were given. After all, you thank other people for their thoughtfulness and consideration toward you, as well as their help, so it is only good manners that you thank your source for the communiqué you received. As you probably know, sincere feelings of gratitude will encourage the receipt of additional pictures, symbols, messages, guidance, and wisdom.

There are television and internet programs that host psychics and mediums and allow them to demonstrate the use of their gift. Watch or listen to these special people because they, too, can be your mentors *if* their words resonate with truth in your "gut instinct" area—the third or Solar Plexus chakra. This is the area where you will "feel the truth" or sense that something said is truth or propaganda.

Practice, practice, and practice using your psychic gift. Trust your "gut instincts," first impression, pictures or symbols, what you hear, and intuition. This is what I did and what many other psychics have done to polish our skills and develop confidence in the use of our wondrous gift.

Remember: close down and cleanse you after your practice sessions!

Chapter 10
Now What?

What do you do with your gift now? You could get more practice at opening up and protecting yourself and then tweak your psychic gift as much as you need to in order to give psychic readings via a "comfortable-for-you" avenue. An avenue such as Astrology—the art of reading a person's birth chart, which is the map of where the planets were at birth and how those planets affect a person.

Palm reading is another avenue. Palm reading is interpreting the lines in a person's hand. Yet another avenue you might want to explore is the reading of Tarot cards, in which you translate the selected cards' messages. Or Rune Stones—a small bag of stones tossed by the person and then the configuration interpreted by the reader. Or Tea Leaves, the art of interpreting the patterns in which the tea leaves lay. Or Numerology—interpreting the birth date and other important date numbers and how those numbers affect a person.

I have chosen to use my psychic gift helping people via the use of astrology, writing, and mentoring those people who are psychic/sensitive/intuitive.

You could use your gift to help the police solve crimes.

With some medical training and chakra energy education, you could use your gift to give energy readings—readings that help find blockages in personal energy, blockages that may create illness.

Or you could use your gift to be a medium—someone who receives messages from those people who have passed over (died) and then gives the messages to the living.

With some additional education, you could become a regression therapist to help heal people who carry wounds or fears from previous lives into this life.

Along with some medical education and training, you could use your gift to help heal animals.

You could become some type of a teacher who uses his/her gift to recognize the psychic gift in children and directs those children in the use of their gift.

With some medical training and chakra energy education, you could become a massage therapist using your gift to find and then help unblock energy for your clients.

You could use your gift to help design and cultivate gardens of fresh food that would feed thousands of people.

Or you could use your gift to perfect meaningful and helpful inventions; a spray-on raincoat or boots that fit in your pocket.

You could use your gift to help paint the most beautiful, realistic pictures anyone has ever seen, or sculpt from marble an Angel wearing a gown that resembles chiffon.

Or you could use your gift in your own life to receive the guidance, wisdom, and inspiration you need to fulfill your life purpose.

Whatever choice you make, be certain to make it with your heart, not from fear—fear that other people may want to use your gift to their advantage, fear of what other people will think of you, or fear of not doing what other people think you should do with your gift.

Using your psychic gift to help other people requires a commitment from you. That commitment is always to give people your very best in a reading and give it from a state of love. So, you do not want to be tired or cranky when you are trying to help someone this way! It requires that you promise yourself always to give people your very best when helping them heal the fears of the past or presenting opportunities for the future. Make sure that you give a person an extra five minutes of your time and an extra spoonful of compassion if the person needs it.

A final thought about your choice of how to use your psychic gift. If you have asked for guidance, cleaned your "hotline," watched and listened for guidance and instruction, and done what you were instructed and guided to do, then whatever choice you have made is the right choice of how to use your psychic gift.

And your decision is the carefully selected choice you and God made together a long, long time ago, and it will resonate as truth to you now. This choice of usage was made long, long ago because the two of you had a tremendous amount of confidence in your spiritual abilities, your willingness to draw on your immense volumes of spiritual wisdom, and your purity of heart.

Respect and honor your decision, love yourself, and cherish your psychic gift. Having, managing, and using your psychic gift in some way is, beyond a doubt, the greatest gift you can give you and the best way to express appreciation to the giver of your psychic gift.

With love, *Miss Dee*

In Conclusion

*E*very morning when you wake up, promise you that you will manage your psychic gift this day and then ask that Angels surround you, protect you, and keep you safe. Now feel the flutter of their beautiful wings hugging you.

Let other people see that beautiful golden liquid-like light twinkling and spinning around you. It is the golden light of self-love, honor, and acceptance.

About the Author

A gifted intuitive herself, Miss Dee mentors people with the psychic gift. When a person learns how to manage the psychic gift, the psychic gift becomes a gift and not a life-long curse of "being an emotional sponge and suffering the constant bombardment of other people's emotions and/or thoughts."

Miss Dee is a certified Esoteric Astrologer and Instructor. She uses her knowledge, wisdom, and expertise to spiritually counsel people using the "amazing tool of astrology along with a lot of T.L.C." to move forward in life and let the past stay in the past.

Miss Dee has written over three hundred astrology and spiritually enlightening articles, and is the author of several books.

She welcomes correspondence via her website,
www.metaphysicians-gallery.com.

www.ingramcontent.com/pod-product-compliance
Lightning Source LLC
LaVergne TN
LVHW051131080426
835510LV00018B/2350